It's a Dachshund Life

Pamela Harry

Prepared for print 2017
HawkMedia
53 Stucley Road
Bideford
Devon
Ex393eq

e-mail: admin@hawkmedia.co.uk
website www.hawkmedia.co.uk

Copyright Pamela Harry

ISBN-13: 978-1981505418
ISBN-10: 1981505415

It's a Dachshund Life
Pamela Harry
All rights reserved
07-12-2017

Description

A poetic celebration of life with dachshunds.

Acknowledgements

Thank you so much to Katy Saxton of 'Penartz Designs' for her very clever illustration for the front cover of my book.

Thank you also to my dachshund loving friends for their support in my writing.

Contents

DACHSHUND ADDICTION	1
MY LONG LOST BROTHER	2
OSCAR'S NEW BOWL	3
TEETHING OSCAR	4
BRUTAL OSCAR	5
NAUGHTY OSCAR	6
DESTRUCTIVE OSCAR	7
AMBER'S BED	8
HARASSED ELSIE	9
AMBER BIRTHDAY GIRL	10
BIRTHDAY BOY LEWIS	11
ELSIE BIRTHDAY GIRL	12
PIPPA ANGEL	13
MUM'S SHADOW	14
MEAL TIMES	15
DANIEL BIRTHDAY BOY	16
DACHSHUND EYES	17
SNATCHER ELSIE	18
TRYING ELSIE	19
DISAPPEARING FURNITURE	20
MOVING DAY	21
OUR VISITORS	22
LETTER FROM JAKE	23
NEGLECTED DACHSIES	24
PARTNERS IN CRIME	25
GERTY	26
LEWIS'S CUSHION	27
GEMMA'S SNUGGLE SACK	28
GEMMA'S WHISKERS	29
CRUFTS	30
MOLLY'S SECRET GARDEN	31
FAT ELSIE	32
GERTY'S HOLIDAY	33
ELSIE'S PUPS	34
NO ORLA	35
ORLA	36
TIRED MUMMY	37
VENUS	38
BUT IT'S RAINING	39
GARDEN HELPERS	40
PUPPY FUN	41
DARCEY'S PUPS	42
OUR HOLIDAY	43
OUR MINI BREAK	44

KIRSTY'S SON	45
THE EDGE	46
NAUGHTY PUPS	47
TISSUE THIEVES	48
GROWN UP ORLA	49
GUILTY	50
FINALE	51

DACHSHUND ADDICTION

Molly was mum's very first
Then Pippa came along
Both of them have left us now
But still mum's love is strong

They started her addiction
No other dog will do
She even did some breeding
So now we're quite a few

There are so many colours
And still she wants two more
She hopes one day she'll breed them
To even up her score

Right now we're at eleven though
So all of you beware
If dachshunds are your favourite dog
You'd best stop at a pair.

MY LONG LOST BROTHER

My name is Sophie
And I've found my handsome brother
Herbert is his name
And Sally is his mother

She saw on social media
That I was so unwell
My birthday was in hospital
Which rang a little bell

Our dates were just the same
And both of us were 6
So contact was then made
And she sent mum Herbert pics

He's such a gorgeous black and tan
And looks so much like me
I wonder now if he recalls
His little sister Sophie

He lives so far away
But it really would be great
If the chance arose for me
To meet my litter mate.

OSCAR'S NEW BOWL

Mum has bought me a new bowl
It's a slow feeder one
Inside it has got bumpy things
To spoil my eating fun

The bottom's got a rubber ring
So won't slide round the floor
But now the others finish first
Can't beat them anymore

I used to have a china dish
But jumped and made it fall
So then it was in pieces
It was a free for all

Mum tried to fight us off
As she needed to clean up
She feared we might eat splinters
I am such a greedy pup

So then I got a metal bowl
But still I'd bolt my meal
No sooner had I finished
I'd be looking whose to steal

But they have all got wise to me
As no one wants to share
And now their noses are in mine
Which I think is unfair

I'm just a little puppy
So I need my food to grow
But once I've had some practice
This feeder won't be slow.

TEETHING OSCAR

My name is Oscar
I'm only 3 months old
But NO is the most common word
That ever I am told

I chewed on my mum's bedding
Despite her saying NO
And now there is a hole in it
As she was just too slow

I chewed paint off the skirting board
And pulled tufts from a mat
And when I chewed the stair carpet
She didn't much like that

I chew on all the garden stuff
And bring in lumps of bark
I chewed on the back doormat
But got the same remark

I chewed the grinder cable
While mum did paws and claws
She shouldn't leave these tempting things
Trailing on the floors

There are boxes in our bedroom
Which were asking to be torn
Inside them is our dog food
But mum just looked forlorn

It seems I cannot ever win
No matter what I do
But I'm a teething puppy
So I've simply got to chew.

BRUTAL OSCAR

Mum is going out today
But I do not agree
As I am not a happy boy
When she goes without me

And so I grab her trouser leg
So that she cannot leave
And when she tries to free herself
I grab hold of her sleeve

And sometimes if I catch her skin
It really makes her yelp
My puppy teeth are just so sharp
But this I cannot help

She tries to walk as I hold on
But I won't ease my grip
And so she has to pick me up
Before her trousers rip

She's also wearing plasters
On the fingers of each hand
As when it comes to treats time
I have to make a stand

If I don't jump in first
Someone else might get my treat
When I'm a growing boy
And I need a lot to eat

So now to save her fingers
Mum tries the closed hand trick
But still I go for others' treats
If I am very quick

She never can be cross for long
As I am far too cute
And no one would believe her
If she said I was a brute.

NAUGHTY OSCAR

Mum says I am a tyrant
A monster and a menace
She thinks instead of Oscar
She should've called me Dennis

If there's something I can't have
It's on my must have list
However much she tells me off
I simply can't resist

I have chewed pens left on tables
And pulled out the DVDs
Chewed on my dad's cookery books
And ripped up all their sleeves

I've had fringe knots off mum's rug
And chewed her coffee table
The rungs on kitchen chair legs
In fact anything I'm able

I've had fun with magazines
And had veggies out the rack
It's great to make a mess
When it's not me who puts it back

The others are all angels
Mum says compared to me
As whenever I'm not sleeping
I am on a wrecking spree

I know she loves me really
But she wants me all grown up
As there is no denying
That I'm such a naughty pup.

DESTRUCTIVE OSCAR

There are holes in mum's trousers
Her tops and nightwear
Holes in her bedding
And her bedroom chair

There are holes now in cushions
And holes in dog beds
Holes in dog blankets
And pulled carpet threads

I've dragged clothes from the dryer
And licked dishwasher plates
I've chewed on dad's paper rack
And chewed both stair gates

The furniture is damaged
The mats and the rugs
But despite my destruction
I still get my hugs

Nothing is safe now
I'm top jumper here
And reach the unreachable
If no one is near

I've chewed on mum's boxes
As she tries to pack
And pulled things from cupboards
When she turned her back

She threatened to pack me
When her wrapping pile fell
I thought I was helping
But she couldn't tell

It seems so much bother
Moving somewhere that's new
But maybe at the next house
There'll be more to chew.

AMBER'S BED

Mum made me my own special bed
Raised up off the floor
My old bed had been getting damp
But now that is no more

I was so very happy
Till others liked it too
They knew it wasn't meant for them
But it was something new

And now they often push me out
Which really isn't fair
We have more beds than dogs here
So I shouldn't have to share

Mum saw what had been going on
And bought another bed
Raised just like my other one
With room for me to spread

I am a standard dachshund
And need more space to sleep
But still they try to pinch what's mine
There's nothing I can keep

So often I'm squeezed into theirs
With mine no longer free
As I am far too soft on them
To let it worry me

But when it comes to night time
The dog bed choice is mine
The minis all pile in with mum
And she then shares with nine.

HARASSED ELSIE

That Darcey is a naughty girl
She keeps on humping me
No matter what mum says to her
She will not leave me be

When minding my own business
She jumps onto my back
And then another jumps on her
To make a 3-way stack

And if our Amber's in this stack
We disappear from view
As she is three times bigger
Than the others in our crew

I don't know what is wrong with them
They're girls the same as me
So why do they then bother
To follow frisky Darcey

It's not her fault she loves me
And others love me too
But when it comes to birds and bees
She hasn't got a clue.

AMBER BIRTHDAY GIRL

My name is Amber
I'm 10 years old today
But still that pesky Darcey
Must annoy me in her way

As soon as it is daylight
She gets up to be fed
And seeks me out to lick my face
While I'm still in my bed

It always makes me grumble
She won't leave me alone
I really ought to snap at her
She loves to make me moan

And when my bark gets louder
Mum scolds her in despair
It happens every morning
But today's a bit unfair

I'm getting on in years now
So this habit needs to break
At least while it's my birthday
Or she'll get no birthday cake.

BIRTHDAY BOY LEWIS

My name is Lewis
I'm 10 years old today
And looking good now for my years
Is what my vet did say

He changed my medication
For seizures from aged 2
And since I'm not so hungry
My weight has dropped off too

I have a lot more energy
Mum smiles at me with pride
I've always been her special boy
Her feelings she can't hide

I play with all the youngsters
And chew on Elsie's ears
It gets me into trouble
But I've done it now for years

I simply cannot help myself
The lure's too great somehow
The chocolates were my favourite
But cream's my craving now

I used to wait for seasons
But Elsie's are sublime
And so if I'm not being watched
I chew them all the time

Today's my special day though
So thoughts are now elsewhere
Of yummy birthday pupcake
For all of us to share.

ELSIE BIRTHDAY GIRL

I'm One! I'm One!
So today's a day for fun
And I am such a big girl now
With my first season done

Mum says when it's the next time
I'll have puppies of my own
But right now I'm the pup still
Even though I look full grown

I wonder what she's got for me
I'm sure new toys are due
There's always room for extras
Though we do have quite a few

And what will be my birthday tea
Smoked salmon or roast lamb
I'm rather fond of eggs as well
Mixed up with beef or ham

Mum makes out all this food's for her
But gives us each a taste
And by the time it's gone round nine
There's nothing left to waste

Everyday at her meal time
We think it's ours as well
And gaze at her with longing eyes
Whilst savouring the smell

She says that I'm a gannet
As I do my best to steal
There's nothing safe when I'm around
What's hers is mine I feel

Sometimes I'm so persistent
I can even make her cross
So have to let her have her way
She likes to think she's boss

We all know in this household though
That mum is here to serve
As after all our good life here
Is just what we deserve.

PIPPA ANGEL

I should have been 11
On this my special day
But I was really poorly
So I had to go away

I know my mummy misses me
And I miss her as well
But still I'm here in spirit
It's just that she can't tell

Everyday she speaks to me
Not knowing that she's seen
And when she does the food bowls
There's a space where mine had been

Sometimes she'll touch the empty space
And softly say my name
I wish she knew that I was near
But it can't be the same

I brush against her trouser leg
When sadness comes from her
I'm sure she'd feel much better
If she just could stroke my fur

One day we'll be together though
Where Molly waits with me
And all of us will have our wings
And share eternity.

MUM'S SHADOW

My name is Gemma
And mum is my best mate
I tolerate her husband
But strangers I just hate

The worst is when she leaves me
And then I hide away
No tempting morsel lures me out
Sometimes I'll hide all day

I give mum such a telling off
She knows I get upset
But cuddles make it better
And help me to forget

We're clued up on the signs though
However hard she tries
The shoes, the purse, the car keys
We've all of us got wise

And so I race to block the door
Protesting all the way
But still she squeezes through the gap
Whilst making sure I stay

And so I am her shadow
And follow everywhere
As sneaking off without me
Is just too hard to bear

And when the others go to bed
I still keep mum in sight
Till finally she scoops me up
To settle for the night.

MEAL TIMES

When we get up for breakfast
The chocolates stay in bed
And only when we've eaten ours
They think they should be fed

First our Tessa wanders in
Followed by our Darcey
But Kirsty waits for hers in bed
Because she thinks she's classy

At tea time she is just the same
Mum's wrapped around her paw
She waits out on the garden bench
As coming in's a bore

Our Gemma's not much better
As she eats away from us
And should we dare to get too near
She'll make the biggest fuss

Amber's bed's her favourite spot
But if she can't have that
She'll go into the hallway
And have it on the mat

And when mum's seen to all of us
It's time to have her own
But even though we've just been fed
We don't leave her alone

We think that she should share with us
Ignoring is unwise
We watch her every mouthful
As we sit with longing eyes

Of course persistence pays
When we always get our way
As meal times in our household
Are much the same each day.

DANIEL BIRTHDAY BOY

My name is Daniel
And I am 5 today
So time for extra spoiling
And for getting my own way

Mum has cut down on my treats
She says I'm overweight
But today these rules must surely change
On this my birthday date

My coat is black and gorgeous cream
I am a stunning boy
But maybe just a little big
Though still mum's pride and joy

But now she's had my bits removed
Which wasn't very fair
No baby Daniels can there be
Without my missing pair

But still I'll love the girlies
And just hope that they love me
Mum said it would be best all round
With less activity

So now I'm always hungry
And my weight is creeping up
She takes me on these great long walks
But I'm a tired pup

It's much more fun to dine on steak
And curl up on mum's bed
I hope that's for my birthday tea
Can't wait till I am fed

I wonder if I'll get new toys
And friends to come and play
Whatever mum has planned for me
I'll have a happy day.

DACHSHUND EYES

Our dachshund eyes are watching mum
To catch her every move
We're ready to create mayhem
If we should disapprove

Because she's putting jackets on
We think she's going out
She says it's getting colder
But we bark on in our doubt

Eventually she calms us down
But she can be quite sly
We've seen her sneak out with the keys
With no word of goodbye

So even if we look asleep
We know what's going on
She needn't try to leave the room
We sense if she is gone

It may just be a bathroom break
But we're not far behind
She never tries to shut us out
So doesn't really mind

And if she sits down in the lounge
To watch what's on TV
We'll pile along the sofa
Once her lap's no longer free

But if she's sitting down with food
Our dachshund eyes fixate
She surely can't then eat it all
Whilst we just sit and wait

We're masters at the starving gaze
We dachshunds love to eat
We don't care if it's ours or mum's
As we deserve a treat

But when she goes into her room
These late hours are the best
We spread ourselves across her bed
And eyes can truly rest.

SNATCHER ELSIE

I'm a greedy treat snatcher
I think they all are mine
No matter who mum tosses to
I always cross the line

I'll grab them from another's mouth
And even from mum's hand
As no one can keep up with me
And no one makes a stand

I know that mummy gets annoyed
Whilst trying to be fair
She doesn't see why I should take
More treats than are my share

Gemma's such a push over
And Kirsty stays away
So mummy feeds the two of them
Whilst holding me at bay

And when it comes to her own meal
I'm barking at her plate
She doesn't always want to share
And I don't like to wait

Because she knows I try to steal
She won't allow me near
She often can be mean like that
But NO I just don't hear

I'm always good at our meal times
And only eat my own
It s just for treats and titbits
That I give mum cause to moan.

TRYING ELSIE

Mum often calls me trouble
But I know that's not my name
As I am really Elsie
The one who gets the blame

If holes appear in flower beds
She knows at once it's me
With dirty paws no longer cream
It seems that I am guilty

And now that we have Autumn leaves
I like to bring them in
But when she sees my shredded bits
She puts them in the bin

We have a box of hooves here
So we can have a chew
But one hoof never is enough
I have to have a few

The same applies to our toy box
I never know which one
And so I get all of them out
Which is so much more fun

And as mum does the clearing up
She says I am a pain
Because when all is put away
I get them out again

To me it's no big deal
When I only want to play
She'd think that I was poorly
If she had a tidy day

So blankets on the floor
From the dog beds upside down
Tell her it's a normal day
With one more cause to frown

She isn't really cross though
As I'll often catch a smile
Because my mummy loves me
Even though I am a trial.

DISAPPEARING FURNITURE

With box piles growing everywhere
There was so little space
But then one of our sofas
Vanished without trace

Strangers came and went
And took our stuff away
Or it went into the garage
But still would go next day

Then came down the sofa bed
As all upstairs was cleared
So now we had a sofa back
But more still disappeared

Worse was yet to come
When our bed base was no more
Just a duvet and our pillows
On our mattress on the floor

It wasn't very long though
Till everything would go
With three strong men in one huge van
To where we didn't know

We all were shut upstairs
So that we could not escape
But when at last we could come down
Our home was in poor shape

The rooms were very empty
No bed for our last night
Just bedding on the carpet
But we managed till first light.

MOVING DAY

Mum gave us our breakfast
And then her final pack
No space was spare inside our car
As we weren't coming back

She drove it to the front gate
So she could load us in
But by mistake dad opened it
Creating such a din

Elsie now was on the loose
But she stayed by the car
Whilst Gemma disappeared from sight
But didn't go too far

Next dad saw a tyre was flat
But still it had some air
He drove us to a garage
And got it pumped up there

We finally were on our way
Mum in the back with us
It really was the tightest squeeze
But no one made a fuss

Dad dropped off our house keys
Before our three hour drive
Delays then with our new keys
Till at last we could arrive

The three strong men were waiting
In their huge van with our stuff
And so we moved from room to room
Unloading time was tough

It was after dark once finished
And the huge van went away
It all was quite chaotic
But mum cleared it day by day

Now it is our dream home
With lots of running space
It really was the hardest move
But worth it for this place.

OUR VISITORS

My name is Sophie
And my brother's come to stay
He brought his best friend Lyla
They were here for Christmas Day

Herbert is his name
It's been eight years since last we met
He was my closest litter mate
By now though we forget

They have a great big bed to share
Just by our bedroom door
There isn't space inside with us
It takes up half the floor

Mostly Lyla sleeps there
In her blanket wrapped up tight
While Herbert's in a bed by mum
For assurance in the night

But with the New Year's fireworks
They came in bed with us
Lyla doesn't like them
And they wanted lots of fuss

They do enjoy our garden
Although Lyla hates the rain
So when mum puts her out to pee
She runs inside again

She loves to chase a squeaky ball
And Herbert likes them too
But all day long she wants them thrown
I think she's lost a few

I'm sure they like our special treats
Cooked chicken and smoked salmon
Roast beef is always welcome
And they loved our Christmas gammon

I know they're going to miss us
Once this holiday is done
But maybe some time later on
They'll have another one.

LETTER FROM JAKE

My name is Jake
I'm a friend from far away
So I guess I'll never meet you guys
But 'Hi from USA'

I am my mom's protector
And an angel in her eyes
I follow everywhere she goes
I'm sure that's no surprise

I've heard of your adventures
From the poems your mum wrote
So mommas mean the world to us
And always get our vote

I love to give mine kisses
In the morning when I wake
But if she wants to stay in bed
It's snuggle time for Jake

I like to stretch across her back
Her neck as my head rest
I know she thinks that's kind of cute
These moments are the best

I also love our morning walks
And gardening's good fun
Especially the wagon rides
Whilst garden chores are done

And when she's sitting in her chair
Reclined with her feet up
Of course I'm settled on her legs
As I'm her pampered pup

We all have our own special ways
I know you have yours too
So even though our paths won't cross
High Paws to all of you.

NEGLECTED DACHSIES

We're such neglected dachsies
Mum has no time for us
Won't someone come to our rescue
So we can get some fuss

First it was the boxes
But now they have all gone
It is the dreaded sewing
With curtains to be done

She says there's only one more room
But we have had enough
These endless days of waiting
Are getting just too tough

She says it hurts her back
So she ought to take a rest
And now she has a horrid cough
So bed would be the best

But still she has to soldier on
Until she felt so ill
She had to lie down for a while
We think she caught a chill

So then she got the message
And today is a day off
But we know she'll get back to it
When she doesn't feel so rough

Of course we get our tasty meals
And always treats galore
But what we need is cuddle time
So waiting's such a bore

She switches on her blanket
To give us her warm bed
But what we want is mum with us
Not sewing things instead

And so we need a rescuer
We've suffered long enough
Mum needs to learn the lesson
We mean more than sewing stuff.

PARTNERS IN CRIME

We're loving our new garden
But Elsie's a naughty pup
And close behind her is Darcey
Trying to dig it all up

The earth here is soft and black
Just perfect for muddy paws
They come in through the utility room
And start treading it all indoors

Mum hoped that a mat and a runner
Would help to keep the floors clean
But when they walk alongside them
Their paw prints are easily seen

Mum scratches her head in despair
As she cleans up the mess once more
But the terrible two refuse to learn
Just what the runner is for

She knows it's a losing battle
And hopes they'll change given time
As these naughty girls are her youngest
And have always been partners in crime.

GERTY

We had a special visit
From Kirsty's litter mate
It was her sister Gerty
Five years since parting date

Mum Tessa kept her distance
But Kirsty said hello
She felt a strong connection
Despite so long ago

We're sure with time together
Their bond would then come back
As pups they were so very close
She'd fit well in our pack

She's also aunt to Darcey
Who too was keen to see
This other chocolate member
Of her chocolate family

We hope if Gerty's mum decides
To take a holiday
She'll come and spend some time with us
We'd love for her to stay

But even just a visit
So again these girls can meet
Tessa's litter was mum's first
Which made it such a treat.

LEWIS'S CUSHION

My name is Lewis
And I have my special place
Between my mummy's pillows
Is my baby cushion space

It's been mine since a puppy
And it's where I sleep at night
Sometimes another pinches it
But then mum puts it right

The cushion has got smaller
Or it might be that I've grown
I've had it for ten years now
So it is my very own

But just as I begin to snore
That Elsie starts to chew
I don't know why she chews on me
I haven't got a clue

It really is annoying
So I grumble and I growl
And then mum turns the light on
And she stops her with a scowl

We all of us have favourite spots
Where best we like to sleep
And though the others envy me
This cushion's mine to keep.

GEMMA'S SNUGGLE SACK

My name is Gemma
And my bed's a snuggle sack
I used to sleep with mummy
But no room now with the pack

And so I choose the kitchen
And Amber's big camp bed
Where lies my comfy snuggle sack
With lots of room to spread

The night is very long though
And I need my bathroom breaks
So I go and visit mummy
Where I paw her till she wakes

And often when she lets me out
Our Sophie comes out too
Elsie needs her breaks as well
And others join the queue

But then a kiss and cuddle
And mum tucks me up once more
Until it's time for breakfast
And more tapping with my paw

I often am too early though
And mum is not impressed
So I'm placed under her duvet
As she claims to need more rest

She says she feels so tired
When she gets a broken night
Perhaps she needs a snuggle sack
To ease her sleeping plight.

GEMMA'S WHISKERS

Mum says I'm growing whiskers
But I am not a cat
And if she thinks to trim them
I'm having none of that

They make me extra special
And not some laughing stock
I think the others envy me
So needn't try to mock

They're cream to match my eyebrows
Though much of me is black
Cream brindle is my colouring
No others in our pack

Maybe mum should curl them
So I look just like a Viking
Everyone would turn their heads
And find me really striking

A dachshund with a moustache
Maybe next I'll grow a beard
But right now I look kind of cute
Whilst that might be quite weird

But mummy loves me anyway
No extra tufts offend
Who cares what others think of me
When I'm her furry friend.

CRUFTS

My name is Kirsty
And Piper is my son
Mum went along to Crufts today
To see what he had won

Sadly it was early
When his time was in the ring
And so my mummy missed him
But he didn't win a thing

Although he's very handsome
He decided to play up
Good looking's simply not enough
If you're a naughty pup

He's done so very well to date
Along with brother Cisko
And once this rebel stage has passed
We hope awards will follow

They've won a lot of rosettes
But a Crufts one would be great
It'll maybe happen next year
Just another year to wait

Either way the owners
Though not the 'best in show'
Always take the best dogs home
Where best is what they know.

MOLLY'S SECRET GARDEN

Mum has made a garden
For Molly's place of rest
With lots of plants for summer
So it soon will look it's best

She built a covered seat
And another one that sways
Now she can sit there peacefully
On sunny tranquil days

She made a water feature
And added gentle chimes
Their sound completes the picture
For pensive quiet times

She even bought a statue
A dachshund made of stone
We thought at first it might be real
Of course we should have known

It seemed to smell of nothing
And didn't move at all
But still it looks so life like
As it sits against the wall

Our Molly's date of birth
Had been Remembrance Day
So a poppy marks her grave
Where we hope she'll always stay

Mum never could forget her
Her introduction to our breed
The start of her addiction
Who'd have thought where it would lead

So many happy memories
But sadness in the end
Still she misses her so much
Her extra special friend.

FAT ELSIE

That Elsie's getting fat
Whatever must she eat
Her tummy's getting very big
You hardly see her feet

Now suddenly she's smaller
A crash diet must have worked
The fat has left her tummy
Or could puppies there have lurked

There seems to be some squeaking
But we're not allowed to see
Mum says that Elsie needs her space
So we must leave her be

Her tummy's hanging down now
You would think she was a cow
We're told that she has lots of milk
But looks so funny now

She's shut in mummy's living room
And just comes out to pee
She doesn't want to play with us
And is grumpy as can be

Mum says she is protective
As her pups are very small
In case we think they're squeaky toys
Which wouldn't do at all

Our Bailey sits beside her gate
He misses her so much
But even when she sees him there
She won't let noses touch

We hope she's back to normal soon
Amongst us in our pack
It's not the same without her
So we want our Elsie back.

GERTY'S HOLIDAY

My name is Tessa
And my daughter's come to stay
She'll be with us for one whole week
Whilst her human is away

Sister Kirsty was excited
But Gerty wasn't sure
And gave her the cold shoulder
Doesn't like her anymore

As puppies they were very close
But five years since have passed
And whilst there seemed to be a bond
The friendship didn't last

I think she likes the others
And will come and sit with me
But Bailey's her new boyfriend
And her favourite plain to see

He's usually with Elsie
But since she's out of bounds
He's glad of the attention
From this newest of the hounds

Mum says that she's no trouble
As she loves her food and sleep
She doesn't bark as much as us
At night there's not a peep

We'll be sad to see her leave
As she's going home today
But I hope my daughter comes again
For another holiday.

ELSIE'S PUPS

I have three little dumplings
So big because of me
They think I am a milk bar
To drain eternally

No sooner have they had their fill
And mum has fed me too
They wake up for some more to drink
So what else can I do

Although they are quite rough now
I take it in my stride
And all of them can see me
As eyes are open wide

They're trying hard to find their feet
And next they'll want to play
So mum will need her bigger pen
In case they climb and stray

I dread the day they get their teeth
It might be time to quit
And hand them over to my mum
As I'll have done my bit

My sleepless nights can then be hers
And I can get some rest
I know that she won't mind though
As these times are her best.

NO ORLA

I think I've learnt a new word
I hear it quite a lot
But being such a good girl
I stop it on the spot

That is until the next time
My memory span is short
But still I know the word now
After giving it some thought

The trouble is a puppy
Can't be good all of the time
If all I was is pretty
How could mum then write this rhyme

It helps of course to look like me
Mum's never really mad
So like my pals before me
I can be a little bad.

ORLA

My name is Orla
Though it could of course be Minx
I've heard mum use them both to me
She gets confused methinks

The rungs on kitchen chair legs
Are just the height for me
To have a little chew on them
Till Minx must leave them be

But when it comes to food time
Orla's what I hear
And when I've eaten all of it
She thinks I am a dear

And out I go then for a pee
So mum heaps me with praise
Until I find more mischief
To while away my days

I love to help with gardening
And leave bits on the lawn
She wouldn't mind if they were weeds
But Minx is said with scorn

How can I tell the difference
When plants all look the same
I hope my brother comes home soon
To take a share of blame

I love it when it's bedtime though
And we all hit the sack
Curled up on mum's bed with her
It's great here in this pack.

TIRED MUMMY

That naughty dog who gets mum up
Has got her up again
Gemma is the culprit
She's really such a pain

Mum hoped for an unbroken night
She got one yesterday
But things are back to normal now
And Gemma likes her way

Because she sleeps with Venus
The newest puppy here
Mum feared that she'd been woken up
Which soon enough was clear

Our Bailey started barking
So Venus then took fright
Mum quickly scooped her up
And took her out into the night

She wouldn't do a pee though
Mum guessed she'd been too late
And sure enough she found one
As poor Venus couldn't wait

A few of us were up then
Pup Orla got up too
Mum put her in the garden
But nothing would she do

So now two pees on carpet
Were mummy's job at 4.00
And two rampaging puppies
Made it such an extra chore

As she trod down paper towels
They grabbed to whip away
And pulled at any corners
Whilst she tried to keep at bay

And when at last she'd finished
And all were back in bed
We soon were soundly sleeping
But mum lay awake instead.

VENUS

My name is Venus
As my real name's 'Sky By Night'
Mum puzzled what to call me
But she thought this one just right

Orla was the baby
But I'm the baby now
But just because she's bigger
She can be a little cow

I can hold my own though
And am growing by the day
So soon I shall catch up with her
And she'll have less to say

We always rough and tumble
But we sleep a lot as well
I think we wear each other out
Creating merry hell

Mum wasn't going to keep me
But I'm sure she's glad I'm here
I m her only silver dapple
So I think she'd shed a tear

If I left her for another home
I know she'd choose the best
But still to me the home I'm in
Is better than the rest

And so I hope that I shall stay
Mum Darcey hopes I do
Orla has her dachshund mum
So I should have mine too.

BUT IT'S RAINING

It's raining I know
But you still have to go
And the place to go is outside
No good rushing in
Or creating a din
Or looking for somewhere to hide

This is the rule
However cruel
And yes I know it is wet
So don't bark at me
It's just water you see
So there's really no reason to fret

Now don't start to howl
I have a soft towel
And soon you'll be warm and dry
It needn't take long
So come on be strong
It's easy if only you'd try

Now come along please
It's dry under trees
And only your paws will get wet
I'll carry you there
To show you I care
But my conditions have to be met

NO not on the mat
It isn't not for that
I've shown you where you should pee
I really despair
Don't you give me that stare
I need you to listen to me

You may think you've won
And think it's good fun
But that's not the way to impress
I'll catch you again
And hope maybe then
We'll finally have some success.

GARDEN HELPERS

My name is Orla
And Ozzie is my brother
He left us once and then came back
But now he's with another

He took with him our Ebony
Then Bruno flew away
But sister Daisy was the first
To disappear one day

Now all that's left is Venus
So she's my playmate new
I'm teaching her to garden
Just as Ozzie used to do

We'd pull up mummy's latest plants
Now Venus has the knack
Mum wasn't at all pleased with us
And had to put them back

Venus is so tiny
But she's growing by the day
And so she's getting stronger
And the bigger plants fall prey

Leaves are stripped and roots are pulled
She nibbles branches too
I can't deny I help her
As they're all so good to chew

We dig holes in the borders
And in the lawn as well
I think our mum has given up
Her look's enough to tell

She knows that we'll grow out of it
She'll sort it out some day
When baby teeth are history
And naughty pups just play.

PUPPY FUN

Time to get dressed
But I'm missing a sock
I find my sock
Now I'm missing a Croc

They're on my shirt
I have to retrieve
As I put on my jacket
They grab a sleeve

I've got my trousers
But have to fight
They have the legs
And hold on tight

I try to walk
They try to grip
More holes I fear
But they soon let slip

Breakfast calls
Now I'm finally free
But first things first
A nice cup of tea

Orla's a piggy
And wants Venus's share
And Venus would let her
If I wasn't there

If she gets a bone
There's one on each end
And always the same toy
To share with her friend

There are many hooves
But both want just one
Typical puppies
But oh so much fun.

DARCEY'S PUPS

I had a boy called Bruno
And a girl called Ebony
But Venus is the one who stayed
To keep me company

Bruno's now in Guernsey
And Ebony's in Kent
And this too is the county
Where Orla's siblings went

But Venus is a bossy pup
Not sure mum's choice was right
She's no respect for others
And could easily cause a fight

She's greedy when it comes to food
And always bolts her meal
And then she's into others' bowls
To see what she can steal

Mostly they will see her off
A grumble is enough
But when it comes to Tessa
She just walks off in a huff

So mummy has to pick her up
Since manners don't abound
Tessa's her great grandmother
A much respected hound

I'm sure she'll learn her place in time
But has a way to go
Sometimes I could disown her
So I hope she's quick to grow

Mummy though adores her
And Orla's very fond
I know that she's my daughter
So of course we share a bond.

OUR HOLIDAY

Mum took us on a holiday
We stayed by Auntie Lynn
She has the biggest caravan
That we could all live in

Our neighbours were two ponies
Ducks and chickens too
And dachshunds in Lynn's garden
Were in our barking view

We had a full length balcony
And steps down to a yard
And as this was our patch now
We stayed on constant guard

We barked at Auntie Lynn
And weren't all very kind
Some left her with their teeth marks
But she didn't seem to mind

Her handyman was scared though
We dachshunds all could sense
He tried to watch for Gemma
And even jumped the fence

We had a comfy double bed
And gave our mum a share
We let her have the very edge
With just enough room there

The kennel dogs woke early
So lots of barking then
But much worse were the cockerels
When they crowed at 4.00am

Mum loved fresh eggs for breakfast
We eyed fresh chicken too
But now that we are home again
We have our own to chew

Of course it's not a real one
They didn't want to play
But maybe we'll return some time
If welcomed back one day.

OUR MINI BREAK

Mum took us all to Devon
Which is so far away
She drove us in her big black car
It was the longest day

We left home in the morning
But 'twas dark when we arrived
Mum worried that we wouldn't cope
But all of us survived

We slept most of the journey
And didn't even pee
And rarely did she hear us bark
We were so good you see

That is until mum parked the car
No longer could we wait
As one by one mum passed us
To a stranger through a gate

Not knowing what was going on
We barked and barked some more
But thankfully the neighbours
Had been warned what was in store

We went into the stranger's house
And mum brought in our stuff
And slowly then we settled down
We think they'd heard enough

And in the time we spent there
We met strangers everyday
So many came to meet us
Mum enjoyed her break away

And Kirsty met her dachshund son
As he's in Devon too
We think at first we scared him
With eleven in our crew

But soon the break was over
And we were homeward bound
It's great to have our bed back though
Where home's a happy hound.

KIRSTY'S SON

I have a chocolate dapple son
And Murphy is his name
But though I saw him recently
He didn't look the same

He's all grown up at 2 years old
So wouldn't have a clue
That we had been connected
But it's possible he knew

He saw us as a family
We came as our big pack
Eleven dogs in total
I think took him aback

He met his sister Darcey
And Tessa is his gran
Our family reunion
From when his life began

And Darcey's daughter Venus
Is related to him too
But she is just a puppy
So to him she is brand new

At first he was quite shy
But he slowly came around
I am so proud of how he's grown
He's such a handsome hound

I don't know if we'll meet again
He lives so far away
Can't tell what's in the future
But it may just be some day.

THE EDGE

We have a comfy kingsize bed
With storage at the end
Covered with soft bedding
To make our bed extend

Of course it's mummy's bed as well
She has to share with nine
She doesn't sleep across like us
One side for her is fine

Kirsty has her pillow
And Darcey's by mum's head
While Tessa likes the storage box
The rest of us just spread

Sophie's under cover
Until she gets too hot
And Orla just wants close to mum
But Elsie wants that spot

And so she squeezes in between
You might say makes a wedge
Until our mum gets pushed
Ever closer to the edge

With no more room to move
She clings on through the night
But then sometimes a falling dream
Will wake her with a fright

She pushes us all over
Annoyed we're in her place
The other side is dog free
But we have to share her space

It's just that we all love our mum
Ignoring her depair
The edge for her is normal
Even if a bit unfair.

NAUGHTY PUPS

Mum isn't at all pleased with us
We're naughty pups you see
We've chewed off her Clematis
At the bottom of it's tree

She'd trained it till it reached the top
But now the twines are dead
She's had to pull it all away
And cut the holding thread

She'd hoped that blossom in the Spring
Would cover it in white
Instead she has bare branches
Which aren't a pretty sight

Maybe it will grow again
And try once more to climb
But looking as it did before
Is bound to take some time

Perhaps she'll buy another
But no flowers will she see
We're sure that she'll protect it though
From our destructive spree.

TISSUE THIEVES

Mum kept on finding tissues
Ripped up on the floor
She'd pick up all the pieces
But then there would be more

She has them in her pockets
To pick up you know what
But sneaky little Venus
Would carefully pinch the lot

Now that mum has caught her out
She thinks she's stopped her game
But Venus is so cunning
She does it just the same

She's even taught our Orla
So now she's joining in
As soon as mum's attention slips
Their mischief can begin

And if it isn't tissues
They bring in lumps of bark
And leaves to shred on carpets
They like to make their mark

It's part of having puppies
These two are not the first
Tissue thieves before them
Have always done their worst

They're growing up so quickly
Mum knows it's just a phase
But then she'll miss their antics
And funny puppy ways.

GROWN UP ORLA

I'm mummy's baby Orla
But I'm a lady pup
I'm having my first season
So I must be all grown up

I'm not yet 8 months old
Mum thought it couldn't be
Suspecting it was Darcey
But she knows now it is me

My dachshund mum just finished hers
Mum's glad when they are done
But since she has another
She fears she'll have a run

With Darcey sure to follow me
And Venus maybe near
She'll be in washing overload
To last her for this year

Christmas should be fun
As we wind up both the boys
I wonder if I'm too mature
To now want Christmas toys

Don't know if I am ready
To give up puppyhood
Don't want to be a lady
And expected to be good

Don't want to be a mother
I want to stay a pup
It's too early for this change of life
Too early for grown up.

GUILTY

We make our mum feel guilty
Each time she tries to eat
Our starving eyes fixated
Especially with meat

We watch her every mouthful
And sit in disbelief
If her food is not on offer
We always give her grief

Young Venus likes to help herself
But mum has now got wise
So doesn't give her half a chance
However hard she tries

We sometimes get to lick her plate
But this to us seems mean
Just being used as prewasher
To make her dishes clean

What we want are morsels
We're sure she has some spare
She claims that we've just eaten
But she gets our hungry stare

Mum knows that it's a battle
Which generally we'll win
Because she is no match for us
And wouldn't want us thin

You can't defy a dachshund
Our begging is a skill
We'll always make you guilty
Should you ignore our will.

FINALE

We hope that you enjoyed our book
And can appreciate
The joy of owning dachshunds
We're sure you just can't wait

To have a dachshund of your own
Or add to what you've got
There's always room to have one more
But great to have a lot.

Printed in Great Britain
by Amazon